This Science Book belongs to

_____

Published by Mindstir Media, LLC
45 Lafayette Rd | Suite 181| North Hampton, NH 03862 | USA
1.800.767.0531 | www.mindstirmedia.com

Printed in the United States of America
ISBN-13: 978-1-7321371-7-2
Library of Congress Control Number: 2018940307

The Apple Experiment

Written by Carol Basdeo

Illustrated by Carl Deris

Acknowledgements

A special thank you to Kate Justine and Mrs. Kamla Bacchus for inspiring and believing in this magnificent project. These amazing women have truly defined friendship. They have proven to me that no distance, near or far, matters if you have friends who truly care about you. I have learned to believe in myself and conquer my fears because I know that the people around me genuinely care about my success.

I was told once that we fall so that we learn how to get up. That statement is ever so true. I am truly grateful for my husband, father, and mother for making my dreams a reality. They have taught me perseverance and to be ambitious because anything is possible through the power of positivity.

To my most treasured and prized possessions, Kayla and K.C., you have motivated and inspired me to explore this brilliant venture. Together we have grown closer and have had so much fun. I am even more inspired to do greatness because I want to leave a better tomorrow for you, my children. I am so proud of the both of you and I love you very much.

On a gloomy Saturday morning, K.C. got up at the crack of dawn. Surprisingly, he even made up his bed. He hurried down to his grandmother's room to watch his favorite cartoon shows.

After a while, he heard his mom calling for him. He ran up the stairs to his mother. He was super excited, hopping from one foot to the other. "Mom! Mom! Guess what?" he shouted, "we have to do the apple experiment today!" His mom was not so crazy about the idea. After all, she had just gotten up.

His mom gestured to him to gather the stuff he needed for his experiment. K.C. laughed, "Silly Mom, that's easy. All we need is water, an apple, and a bowl." As he led the way to the kitchen, he turned to his mom, "Mom, I need your help. I have the apple, but I can't reach the bowl." Lazily, his mom went into the kitchen and handed K.C. a bowl.

By this time, K.C. had made enough of a racket to wake up his sister, Kayla. Kayla yawned her good morning. She asked, "What are you guys doing?"

"My apple experiment," said K.C. with excitement sparkling in his eyes.

At K.C.'s request, Mom helped fill the bowl on the kitchen counter with water while Kayla watched. K.C. dropped the apple into the bowl. Splash! There was water on the countertop. "Oops! Sorry!" said K.C. They all giggled. The apple popped up to the surface of the water.

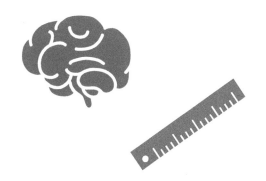

K.C. asked, "Hey guys, do you know why the apple is floating?" They both shook their heads. K.C. proudly explained, "The apple floats because it is less dense than the water."

"Oh, that's neat!" said Mom and Kayla at the same time with a smile

"Hey K.C. what does dense mean?" asked Kayla.

K.C. replied, "Density is when the particles of an object are packed closely together, so the apple is less dense."

Both kids shouted, "We love science!"

Join us next time for another
fun science adventure.

See you soon!

CPSIA information can be obtained
at www.ICGtesting.com
Printed in the USA
BVHW02n1740110518
515778BV00003B/43/P